WEEKLY WR READER®
EARLY LEARNING LIBRARY

**Animals That Live in the Mountains/
Animales de las montañas**

Golden Eagles/
Águila real

by/por JoAnn Early Macken

Reading consultant/Consultora de lectura:
Susan Nations, M.Ed.,
author/literacy coach/consultant in literacy development
autora/tutora de alfabetización/
consultora de desarrollo de la lectura

Please visit our web site at: www.garethstevens.com
For a free color catalog describing Weekly Reader® Early Learning Library's list
of high-quality books, call 1-877-445-5824 (USA) or 1-800-387-3178 (Canada).
Weekly Reader® Early Learning Library's fax: (414) 336-0164.

Library of Congress Cataloging-in-Publication Data

Macken, JoAnn Early, 1953-
    [Golden eagles. Spanish & English]
    Golden eagles = Águila real / by JoAnn Early Macken.
      p. cm. — (Animals that live in the mountains = Animales de las montañas)
    Includes bibliographical references and index.
    ISBN 0-8368-6450-6 (lib. bdg.)
    ISBN 0-8368-6457-3 (softcover)
    1. Golden eagle—Juvenile literature. I. Title: Águila real. II. Title.
  QL696.F32M253   2006
  598.9'423—dc22   2005033305

This edition first published in 2006 by
Weekly Reader® Early Learning Library
A Member of the WRC Media Family of Companies
330 West Olive Street, Suite 100
Milwaukee, WI 53212 USA

Managing editor: Valerie J. Weber
Art direction: Tammy West
Cover design and page layout: Kami Strunsee
Picture research: Diane Laska-Swanke
Translators: Tatiana Acosta and Guillermo Gutiérrez

Picture credits: Cover, pp. 5, 9, 13, 17 © Tom and Pat Leeson; p. 7 © Yuri Shibnev/
naturepl.com; pp. 11, 19 © Alan & Sandy Carey; p. 15 © Niall Benvie/naturepl.com;
p. 21 © John Downer/naturepl.com

Printed in the United States of America

2 3 4 5 6 7 8 9 10 10 09 08 07 06

Note to Educators and Parents

Reading is such an exciting adventure for young children! They are beginning to integrate their oral language skills with written language. To encourage children along the path to early literacy, books must be colorful, engaging, and interesting; they should invite the young reader to explore both the print and the pictures.

Animals That Live in the Mountains is a new series designed to help children read about creatures that make their homes in high places. Each book describes a different mountain animal's life cycle, behavior, and habitat.

Each book is specially designed to support the young reader in the reading process. The familiar topics are appealing to young children and invite them to read — and reread — again and again. The full-color photographs and enhanced text further support the student during the reading process.

In addition to serving as wonderful picture books in schools, libraries, homes, and other places where children learn to love reading, these books are specifically intended to be read within an instructional guided reading group. This small group setting allows beginning readers to work with a fluent adult model as they make meaning from the text. After children develop fluency with the text and content, the book can be read independently. Children and adults alike will find these books supportive, engaging, and fun!

— Susan Nations, M.Ed., author, literacy coach,
and consultant in literacy development

Nota para los maestros y los padres

¡Leer es una aventura tan emocionante para los niños pequeños! A esta edad están comenzando a integrar su manejo del lenguaje oral con el lenguaje escrito. Para animar a los niños en el camino de la lectura incipiente, los libros deben ser coloridos, estimulantes e interesantes; deben invitar a los jóvenes lectores a explorar la letra impresa y las ilustraciones.

Animales de las montañas es una nueva colección diseñada para presentar a los jóvenes lectores algunos animales que viven en regiones montañosas. Cada libro explica, en un lenguaje sencillo y fácil de leer, el ciclo de vida, el comportamiento y el hábitat de un animal de las montañas.

Cada libro está especialmente diseñado para ayudar a los jóvenes lectores en el proceso de lectura. Los temas familiares llaman la atención de los niños y los invitan a leer — y releer — una y otra vez. Las fotografías a todo color y el tamaño de la letra ayudan aún más al estudiante en el proceso de lectura.

Además de servir como maravillosos libros ilustrados en escuelas, bibliotecas, hogares y otros lugares donde los niños aprenden a amar la lectura, estos libros han sido especialmente concebidos para ser leídos en un grupo de lectura guiada. Este contexto permite que los lectores incipientes trabajen con un adulto que domina la lectura mientras van determinando el significado del texto. Una vez que los niños dominan el texto y el contenido, el libro puede ser leído de manera independiente. ¡Estos libros les resultarán útiles, estimulantes y divertidos a niños y a adultos por igual!

— Susan Nations, M.Ed., autora/tutora de alfabetización/
consultora de desarrollo de la lectura

Golden eagles build huge nests. Each year, they add more sticks. Baby eagles, or **eaglets**, hatch in the nests.

-- -- -- -- -- -- -- -- -- -- -- -- -- --

Las águilas reales hacen nidos enormes. Cada año añaden nuevos palitos. Las crías de águila, o **aguiluchos**, salen de los huevos en el nido.

eaglet/
aguilucho

5

An eaglet has soft feathers called **down**. Its father brings it meat to eat. Its mother feeds it small pieces.

Un aguilucho tiene unas plumas suaves llamadas **plumón**. Su padre trae carne para alimentarlo. Su madre se la va dando en pequeños trozos.

Eagles start to fly in about three months. They fly and hunt during the day. At night, they rest in trees.

Las águilas comienzan a volar, más o menos, a los tres meses. Durante el día, vuelan y cazan. Por la noche, descansan en los árboles.

9

Golden eagles have gold feathers on their heads and necks. Feathers cover their legs. The feathers look like boots.

— — — — — — — — — — — — — —

Las águilas reales tienen plumas doradas en la cabeza y el cuello. Las patas están cubiertas de plumas. Esas plumas parecen unas botas.

11

A golden eagle can hear well. It listens for other eagles. It listens for storms. If an eagle gets wet, it may not be able to fly.

El águila real puede oír muy bien. Puede oír a otras águilas. Puede oír la llegada de una tormenta. Si un águila se moja, podría tener problemas para volar.

An eagle may fly many miles to find food. A golden eagle soars over the mountains. It can spot a rabbit from far away.

Un águila puede llegar a volar muchas millas en busca de comida. Un águila real planea sobre las montañas. Es capaz de ver a un conejo desde muy lejos.

15

Eagles dive from the sky. They strike their prey with their feet. They catch their prey with their claws, or **talons**.

- - - - - - - - - - - - - - - - - - -

Las águilas descienden en picado desde el cielo. Golpean a su presa con las patas. La atrapan con sus uñas, o **garras**.

talons/garras

Eagles have strong hooked bills. They tear their prey apart. Golden eagles hunt rabbits and rodents. They also eat lizards and birds.

－－－－－－－－－－－－－－－－－

Las águilas tienen picos ganchudos y fuertes. Despedazan a sus presas. Las águilas reales cazan conejos y roedores. También comen lagartos y aves.

bill/pico

19

In winter, golden eagles may fly to warmer places to find food. They follow their prey down the mountains. In spring, they fly back up.

-- -- -- -- -- -- -- -- -- -- -- -- -- -- --

En el invierno, las águilas reales pueden volar a lugares más cálidos en busca de comida. Siguen a sus presas a zonas más bajas. En la primavera, las águilas reales regresan a las montañas.

Glossary

bills — beaks

prey — an animal hunted for food by another animal

rodents — animals with teeth that keep growing, such as rats, mice, and squirrels

soars — flies or glides high in the air

strike — to hit

Glosario

golpear — dar un golpe

pico — parte de la cabeza de las aves

planear — volar a gran altura

presa — animal devorado por otro animal

roedores — animales cuyos dientes crecen sin parar, como ratas, ratones y ardillas

For More Information/Más información

Books

Eagles. Patrick Merrick (Child's World)

Eagles. Deborah Hodge (Kids Can Press)

Libros

El águila americana. Lynda Sorensen (Rourke)

*Águilas, nopales y serpientes/Eagles, Prickly Pear Cactus
    Pads and Serpents.* Claudia Burr (Planeta Publishing)

Web Sites/Páginas web

Shadow Over the Sun: A Story of Eagles
Una sombra sobre el Sol: Una historia de águilas

www.pbs.org/wnet/nature/shadow
Golden eagle photos, facts, and resources
Fotografías de águilas reales, información y recursos

Index

Índice

About the Author

JoAnn Early Macken is the author of two rhyming picture books, *Sing-Along Song* and *Cats on Judy*, and more than eighty nonfiction books for children. Her poems have appeared in several children's magazines. A graduate of the M.F.A. in Writing for Children and Young Adults Program at Vermont College, she lives in Wisconsin with her husband and their two sons.

Información sobre la autora

JoAnn Early Macken ha escrito dos libros de rimas con ilustraciones, *Sing-Along Song* y *Cats on Judy*, y más de ochenta libros de no ficción para niños. Sus poemas han sido publicados en varias revistas infantiles. JoAnn se graduó en el programa M.F.A de Escritura para Niños y Jóvenes de Vermont College. Vive en Wisconsin con su esposo y sus dos hijos.